A HANDBOOK FOR WRITERS

BY VERN RUTSALA

The Window (1964)
Small Songs (1969)
The Harmful State (1971)
Laments (1975)
The Journey Begins (1976)
Paragraphs (1978)
The New Life (1978)
Walking Home from the Icehouse (1981)
The Mystery of Lost Shoes (1984)
Backtracking (1985)
Ruined Cities (1987)
Selected Poems (1991)
Little-Known Sports (1994)
Greatest Hits 1964-2002 (2002)
A *Handbook for Writers* (2004)

A HANDBOOK FOR WRITERS

Vern Rutsala

WHITE PINE PRESS • BUFFALO, NEW YORK

ACKNOWLEDGMENTS: Thanks to the editors of the following publications in which some of the new work printed here originally appeared:
Calapooya: "Avalanches," "Manifesto," "What Shall We Do?"; *The Chariton Review*: "The Shop Steward," "Friendship: A Fable," "Plagiarism," "The House You Lost," "The Old Man and the Menu"; *Denver Quarterly*: "Our Sad Garden," "Whistle Stop," "The House of Your Dream"; *5 AM*: "The House of Usage"; *Hubbub*: "Night Games," "One Kind of Pain," "Approaching 1934"; *Mississippi Review*: "Hardyesque"; *Models of the Universe: An Anthology of the Prose Poem*, Stuart Friebert, David Young, eds., Oberlin College Press: "House of Cards," "Reunion: A Scenario"; *The Prose Poem*: "Hannelore" ; *River City*: "Luck"; *The Seattle Review*: "Our Mystery."

The selected work previously appeared in: *The Harmful State*, ©1971, Best Cellar Press; *Paragraphs*, ©Vern Rutsala 1978, Wesleyan University Press; *Little-Known Sports*, ©Vern Rutsala, 1994, University of Massachusetts Press.

Thanks also to the editors of the following publications in which the selected work originally appeared: *The American Poetry Review, Antenna, Chicago Review, The Dragonfly, The Greenfield Review, The Iowa Review, kayak, The Mississippi Review, Pendragon, Poetry NOW, Portland Review, The Quarterly Review of Literature, The Reaper, Seneca Review, Stand* (England), *Writing Poetry*, Barbara Drake, ed.

Cover drawing by Vern Rutsala

First Edition

Library of Congress Control Number: 2003116769

ISBN: 1-893996-72-7

Printed and bound in the United States of America
The Marie Alexander Poetry Series, number , 7
Edited by Robert Alexander

The publication of this book has been made possible by support from Robert Alexander, the National Endowment for the Arts, and with public funds from the New York State Council on the Arts, a State Agency.

White Pine Press
P.O. Box 236
Buffalo, NY 14201

www.whitepine.org

CONTENTS

from PARAGRAPHS

from LITTLE-KNOWN SPORTS

The Art of Photography and Other Sorrows

Bestiary

Little-Known Sports

Writing is easy. All you have to do is stare at a blank sheet of paper until drops of blood form on your forehead.
—Gene Fowler

I was working on the proof of one of my poems all morning, and took out a comma. In the afternoon I put it back.
—Oscar Wilde

Manuscript: Something submitted in haste and returned at leisure.
—Oliver Herford

If you want to make God laugh, make plans.
—Yiddish Proverb

The profession of letters is, after all, the only one in which one can make no money without being ridiculous.
—Jules Renard

A work in which there are theories is like an object which still has its price-tag on it.
—Proust

I feel every morning that I am on trial for my life and will not be acquitted.
—Van Wyck Brooks

Works of art are of an infinite loneliness, and nothing so little as criticism can reach them.
—Rilke

You have to be strong in the legs to write.
—Thoreau

TO JOAN

A HANDBOOK FOR WRITERS

AVALANCHES

For centuries the snows waited, winter after winter, while steadily gathering in large pendant masses that hibernated through eons. Though immensely patient they felt they had no purpose and considered themselves to be little more than enormous oafs, filled with self-loathing. What could they do, after all? But then all their pent-up energy found its outlet when mountain climbing and skiing became popular activities.

CHEKHOVIAN

In the provincial village of A—the rain falls on a desolate dog waiting for his master outside a tavern. The dog—Misha—has the thin whiskers of a minor clerk at the local ministry. In fact his master is just such a clerk and is now weeping quietly on a rough bench in an ill-lit corner of the smoky tavern. He has been passed over for promotion for the fifth time and now knows that all is lost and that it is only a matter of time before his superior will tell him flatly that his unsatisfactory service is no longer needed. In spite of this he is spending his last ruble on vodka which he dilutes with his tears. Everyone else in the bar, huddling and shivering in their nondescript scarves and fraying coats, laughs at him, their own miserable lives momentarily lightened by his open display of weakness.

WHAT SHALL WE DO?

What shall we do with this sadness, this enormous untrained pet, this giant sheepdog hippo lumbering through our china shop or always curled in a favorite chair wolfing rubber plants, a mass smothering our bed. We must be kind to animals—the warranty insists —but what do we do with this blind presence which is always always always there. And god how it eats! Peanut butter and jelly sandwiches, French fries, ice-cream. It snuffles around while we sleep, snorting and farting. It acts as if it owns the place, this great shaggy sorrow. Its whimpers of hunger make us want to cry but the Humane Society must be called. We have a large box ready. We will go quietly.

THE HOUSE OF USAGE

Here, in these dusty halls your words fester like keepsakes kept so long you've forgotten what they are and why on earth you saved them so long. And from some inner rift in usage something apologetic sifts into your language and your verbs kowtow, your nouns tug their forelocks—this world wants no person, place, or thing of yours. It hungers for the almost, the sort of, the, you know, *like*...

MANIFESTO

It is time to stop all this politeness toward BMWs and Mercedes. There need to be checks and balances, after all. We also need to reduce the vitality of some of our statistics—some of them have gotten truly out of hand. And henna? Isn't there enough of it around already? We've also noted lately that there is entirely too much attention paid to sturgeon. This must stop. And what about the arrogance of dentists? Or shoe-strings that break only when you are late for an appointment? There is much to be done—about this fetishism of the semi-colon, for example. Some of us are really upset. And what should be done with the deification of the mock turtle? It is certainly time we stopped biting our tongues—they're already flimsy as old lace. Isn't it time as well that counterfeiting was officially recognized as an art form?

TO BORGES

I, too, had my tigers, Jorge, but mine did not come from books or a zoo—our town was too poor for a zoo. Perhaps I saw one in a movie I've forgotten. Whatever their source I had my tigers—their razor teeth dripping saliva and blood, those gaping mouths aimed at my side, those giant claws ready to pin me down. When I was four they arose from my pillow every night for a month, filling me with absolute terror every time I tried to sleep. Unlike you I have never tried to dream them back because I am afraid they would come.

HOW WE GET BY

By hook or crook, by shoestring and bootstrap, by running and hiding, by mortice and tenon, by moving under cover of darkness, by wit and dumb luck, by spit and polish, by weights and measures, by love or money, by hurrying up and waiting, by word of mouth, by bread and board, by slice and dice, by not letting the left hand know, by bed and breakfast, by nuts and bolts, by nodding and smiling, by mortar and pestle, by hammer and tongs, by never crying over what we spill, by backing and filling, by surf and turf, by health and safety, by soup and sandwich, by bourbon and water, by offense and defense, by being as dumb as an ox is strong, by mind and body, by day for night, by sturm and drang, by fire and ice, by hit or miss—oh yes, by hit or miss.

MY NEW PEN

I have been given an expensive pen—it is quite beautiful and feels almost too comfortable in my hand. Words flow freely from it but they seem a little odd, almost alien, as if they belonged to the pen and not to me. This is why I hesitate and worry when I pick up the pen. Is there something counterfeit about the words this pen allows me to write? Or is it simply that I am not good enough for this pen and it is demonstrating this to me? The words that come are certainly quite elegant and even have a touch of the aristocratic about them. That is definitely not me! I who, as they say, was born with a greasy spoon in my mouth. But it is such a beautiful pen! Finally, though, it is a snob which is why I have written this with a cheap ballpoint I filched from the office.

NIGHT GAMES

In the deep winter dark the dead relax, take out the old pinochle deck—loving the greasy feel of the ancient cards—and play for hours. They care about winners and losers, but not much, and some just kibitz a while or wander off and watch us sleep. But our sleep is such a poor imitation of what they do that they get bored and practice a little mischief by making burglar sounds at the windows or by sending skittery noises through the walls. You might think the old family albums would draw their interest but they know all that far too well, existing as they do in a kind of perpetual sepia. Some read the papers, checking the box scores or the recent obituaries, or even pore over new books. But they grow impatient and shuffle toward the card game where they take seats, at ease until they feel the approach of morning.

THERE IS...

There is a nearness you can never touch. It is like a lost memory—the kind you value so greatly just because it's lost—like the softness of your mother's cheek. This nearness lives in those caves inside music, those places where you sink and rise in those tunes that break your heart. It is the minus of far, the active voice of never, the wind's apostrophe. At night in the backyard in summer you feel it in the highest branches where birds sleep and wait like emcees to announce the dawn and where you sometimes nearly catch the feathery nearness just as you wake up.

THE SHOP STEWARD

We had a solid contract to keep moving the stone up the hill as long as anyone wanted—it was dull but steady work. But the gods—given to whims as they are—locked us out, bent on breaking our union. Oh you never read about this, how we threw up a picket line, how the gods sent in a squad of goons to beat us bloody. But we hung on as long as we could until they hired that scab, Sisyphus.

FRIENDSHIP: A FABLE

It works this way: You are invited into her parlor and served tea and mushroom and spinach dishes. The talk is sweeter than the jelly; the butter for muffins won't melt in her mouth. Sated and apparently loved— or at least liked—you relax and feel expansive until you suddenly realize that she is the spider and you, poor fool, are the fly.

ONE KIND OF PAIN

Our nights are too long—we don't have dreams enough to fill them. Near morning they sag like empty bags—a kind of slack agony the right size for lunches. As in most things it's the missing ingredients that make the difference. Without them our pain is strange and private, almost an acquired taste. What isn't there is what we eat and thus we go to bed hungry too many nights. Our sleep needs a nourishment we cannot find; thus we wake every morning to starvation and carry it to work in our brown bags of emptiness.

THE HOUSE OF PLEASURE

Your hand tastes the doorknob and hears the lovely cries of the mullioned windows. Inside, the light is like perfume and caresses your skin as your bare feet listen to the rich carpet murmuring endearments. Each object is built of whatever material you crave—the smell of coffee, the texture of sea breeze—and the sheets on the beds have lovers woven into their sweet fabrics.

CONVERSATION PIECE

There remain nights like this when we fall in love with vacancy; when we need the grinding sound of wreckage and see hope float toward seawrack; nights when we're more than half in love with easeful death turning violent as crazy boulders applauding their own avalanche. We look then for some battered darkness, some oblivion reached by way of pain, some rock-bottom abrasive with sandpaper and broken bones, some exit from this still night, this calm evening with its administrative version of the world.

OUR MYSTERY

The first signs are small: Phones ringing too long, lights left burning all night, shades kept down all day. Then we saw strange cars by the curb and once a door hung open all one morning, moving slightly in the wind. Next, vacancy signs, estate sales, and tall men in black suits. We thought of plants going brittle and pets left to starve in cellars, of friends lost for good in old address books. And today we felt a presence grinning like a salesman, some cloaked figure sent among us to spoil second honeymoons or handcuff standing ovations for the neighbor who screams, "But I'm eighty years young!" It haunts with corn plaster and hiccups, it chokes with loopholes and fine print, it comes to rub winks right out of the eyes of couples married fifty years or five. Ghost towns shuffle in its wake.

PLUME REVISITED

Plume's wife said, "You've been looking rather out of sorts lately and I've made an appointment with my doctor. Be sure to be on time—he is very impatient."

Plume thought there was a pun there somewhere—about a doctor being impatient—but he couldn't get hold of it. Oddly enough he was feeling quite well, fully recovered from last year's ailments—that dangling participle, for instance. But he had a great respect for the medical profession and agreed to go.

Though he arrived at the doctor's building in good time Plume could not find the office because there was no directory nor were there any names on the doors. He opened a door and a naked man screamed at him while making come-hither gestures and he quickly slammed the door shut. Behind the next door there appeared to be only a large tank full of lazy looking fish.

Eventually he found the doctor's office and, my, was the doctor angry. "I am a very busy man and you've already taken up too much of my valuable time. Besides I only gave you an appointment because of your wife—she's a real tootsie, isn't she?" At this the doctor shot his eyebrows up and down rapidly in a manner made famous by Groucho Marx.

"Please take off those unsightly clothes at once!" the doctor said, tapping his foot, and Plume complied quickly, so quickly that he pulled two buttons off his shirt while wondering why his outfit was unsightly. After all his wife had picked it out for him especially to suit her doctor.

The doctor then spun Plume around and gave him a swift karate chop to the throat and forced his left arm into a painful hammerlock. Gasping, Plume said in a hoarse voice, "What are you doing?"

"Don't ask questions! I'm the doctor here. I'm just testing your flexibility. But what about that voice of yours? It sounds very bad."

"But you just hit me—" Plume said with effort.

"Nonsense. That was therapeutic. Now open your mouth, let's see that ugly throat of yours."

"Oh, yes," the doctor said after forcing a large tongue depressor that looked like a swagger stick down Plume's throat.

"Do you drink, smoke, eat bagels with lox?" the doctor said.

"How am I supposed to answer three questions at once?" Plume rasped out, gently touching his neck.

"Yes no and all."

"But,"—at this the doctor jammed the depressor down Plume's throat until he gagged rather pathetically.

The doctor then called to his nurse for a scalpel and a trachial tube and after slicing open Plume's throat he quickly inserted the tube. "That will help you breathe. This is one of the worst cases I've ever seen."

Unable to speak, Plume wondered what it was a case of, but the profuse bleeding from the wound made him feel slightly woozy.

"Now let's have a look at that arm," the doctor said, wrenching it hard, and before Plume could even blanch the doctor sliced it off at the shoulder. "I love these new scalpels," he said to the nurse, who beamed.

In no time the doctor had reduced Plume to little more than a bloody torso and said, "This will make a new man of you." As he spoke he eyed Plume's genitals and the poor man fainted.

Plume's widow was very grateful for the doctor's

aggressive efforts and even wrote a testimonial expressing her flowery and profuse thanks. The doctor framed it and put it on his wall.

i.m. Henri Michuax

THE HOUSE OF CARDS

The first rule: It must stand all evening. Tonight, you have obeyed that rule and the house of cards still stands. You close the door gently and the cool night air, the sure beams of the headlights, the sensible direction home all rejoice quietly but with restraint, like cricket fans. And it is now, faced with the ordered desolation of your own rooms, that you know it has come to this: You who began as an animal, who should have been at the very least a pirate—you have come to rejoice when nothing happens, when you make no more imprint on an evening than a bare foot on thick grass, when you have absolutely nothing to remember.

OUR SAD GARDEN

Our garden is made of words—each leaf written down. First in everyday English and then in Latin. Either way it means nothing. Either way it goes to seed and we turn away feeling a weakness behind our knees—that feeling you have when your child's in danger, only slower, sadder, the weakness moving down our calves like sap.

Thus we turn away from our sad garden of words in two languages, the failed garden, the garden of no earthly delights, our chosen garden, our victory garden come to this wild nonsense of weeds and briars, broken syllables, the writings of the illiterate spreading out and away forever.

WHISTLE STOP

Your phantom cousins sleep in this town.

GOOD GUESTS

We sit in a room armored by light and surrounded by surfaces bright as mirrors. Everything shines and gives comfort, nothing is out of place and our hosts, too, are immaculate, each hair placed with the skill of a jeweler. Our words flutter and fail, too dusty, while theirs flow out in perfect paragraphs. We wonder why they invited us, disheveled and in tatters as we are, to enter their lives. Should we confess our unworthiness? And oh we want to scour our brains for some small accomplishment but find nothing worthy, nothing to equal the gleaming parquet of their smiles. They are so well-bred we can't believe our good luck, all our gnarled deceits brought here to be honored! And then, suddenly, we know: They're specialists to whom we've come with our shabby guilts and petty crimes to be killed with exquisite kindness.

NOW

Sudden anger fills the house—plants curl up, leaves droop, the dream you were planning to have tonight declares itself ineligible. Warm rooms go cold and now you see each chewed edge of rug, every dusty corner asserts its rights, the old house sagging down toward its vision of vacant lots. And you, too, want to give up and join dust and sag, give all your change away— those small hopes! That pocket music!—and fall down before the smithereens of rage—the sky is falling! The sky is falling!

THE HOUSE OF SPEECH AND HUNGER

A voice from the cellar says it's hungry, and famine cries from the dark carbohydrates of the world. In the vastness of malnutrition each house longs for its mate—are the semi-detached happier than the detached? But it's hard to speak of love, your house says. What do I know? Wind and rain write critiques on my roof and the great clouds roll over me like abandoned sleeping bags.

LOCAL GAME

We're all-round players of this game—offense, defense, we go both ways. Watch us some time—have popcorn and a beer, no program needed. Watch as we attack, watch hurt rise in the other's eyes. Watch us bite bullets and lips but never our tongues. See the first tear or the fist against the wall. See the chair throw or, better, the dishes on the floor—the one with the most broken pieces wins. This is our Olympics. We're adept and on a streak. We never quit though we do take time out for guilt or the pleasure of licking wounds. The virtues of our sport? You're never too old and every game finally ends with two losers.

STORM

Our latest myth is storm and we hear it looping down the flue to stir our ashes, hear the gunshot crack of splitting branches, the spit and hiss of broken power lines as they release their sap as our big tree trembles like a fern. All over town shingles give in to
their secret ambition to become kites. We move to distant cliffs, the sea roiling below, boats chopped to kindling on the rocks. We love this version of the world ringing true all night, impossible to counterfeit.

THE HOUSE OF SLEEP

It has an obscure address with the streets leading there lined with worry and old embarrassments wincing from hoardings. You have to pass a field of sheep which you are obliged to count of course before you move on. But it's a modest herd and if you continue you will find the house of sleep welcoming. Within it all things sleep deeply—the aspect of a chair's siesta is comforting as are the dreaming mirrors, surfaces so calm as if all the secrets had long ago drifted to the bottom and lie there in the deep fathoms of a coma.

THE OLD MAN AND THE MENU

The light was good and he liked the smooth feel of the carte in his hands and he held it casually and with grace. Having sharpened twenty pencils, he was ready and read the list from beginning to end and felt saddened because there was no more to read. At this point he weighed himself and counted the words on the menu. The leaves on the surrounding trees were green and he knew he would read the list again and knew it was necessary not to become overly excited if he expected the earth to move when the food was served. He concentrated hard and then struck the menu with his open palm and ordered the fish and chips.

HOW IT FEELS

Tonight we taste rust in the weather and there is some helpless deep shrug in our strata. But something worse has already happened and we wander around the aftermath of debris, the marketplace of disease. Or perhaps we only imagine this as we drink our immaculate wine and only think we discover deep mouth-like fissures devouring all the twisted artifacts we pay and pay for, all these inedible things we taste while our genteel blood slows and congeals and we share out the lovely brie of our loneliness.

THE WALKER IN THE HOUSE

Awake all night I sleep all day, alone in the house, vaguely hearing that casual searcher wandering downstairs as he shops through the rooms, finding each floorboard that speaks, fingering dim music from the silverware, idly dialing the phone, skimming books, clinking empty glasses in silent toasts. All day he conducts his tour studying the things of my life casually, at leisure, and then disappears in the air when I wake up remembering some blurred visitor in my dreams who was lost for good behind the closing door I think I heard just now.

VERBS

They come in a variety of sizes—the large muscular ones somewhat like Picasso's huge-bodied and pinheaded athletes but there are also the quiet and passive milquetoasts who seem to seek nothing more than anonymity. We are taught, of course, to favor the athletes who at their best can give language pace and verve but at their worst may be as bogus and full of false bravado as professional wrestlers.

PLAGIARISM

The average practitioner makes the mistake of simply copying out passages while the somewhat more skillful takes the trouble to lace his theft with a few errors—misspellings and erratic punctuation and so on. On a still more sophisticated level are those who paraphrase without citing their sources, but the real masters are those who produce work which is at times far superior to the originals, work which is, in fact, an exquisite forgery.

THE HOUSE OF YOUR DREAM

I enter your house with stealth, making sure I'm dressed properly—checking buttons, the shine on my shoes—trying to look normal because you say your dreams are so ordinary and I don't want to stand out. You say you spend your dreams packing and shopping, engaging in small talk. But inside your dream I notice a strange light, the light that colored your childhood, and your suitcases are covered with exotic stickers. The very streets you windowshop along are unlike any streets I remember—each store a museum of the mysterious, each window faceted like a diamond. I follow a few paces behind you as you buy tea and apples—the tea seems alive with the sounds of India and each apple has a window where families look out and wave. Each object you meet glows with that old light, even the sidewalk looks like a rainbow— because it is your dream and I am a stranger here.

LUCK

You carry a broken mirror in your pocket like a rabbit's foot and refuse to call the days by their right names, assuming your way out is self-indulgence and that somehow the spirit loves best those who use themselves hard, readily submitting to ordeals of fire and ice. Thus you court the danger of seven years' bad luck and fiddle with the edge of total loss on the thinnest ice you can find. For example, some nights you begin driving at the speed limit and then go faster; other nights Billie Holiday's dying voice makes you dance a tarantella on all the sidewalk cracks of your mother's back.

Now this is touchy stuff with "why's" lurking everywhere. All answers are murky. Failure isn't really the aim—as in an athlete's secret quest for awkwardness or beauty's courtship of the beast. In part it's dumping shaker after shaker of salt and never throwing a single grain over your shoulder; it's calling every night Saturday night; it's keeping the rabbit and throwing the foot away, assuming this is what the spirit loves, hearty and devil-may-care. Your campaign, finally, is against the good taste of the world as well as the nail without hammer, nest without bird, mouth without food. You go your own way with great pleasure, ordering everything on the menu, staying everywhere until closing time, then driving fast to find the perfect after-hours joint, your standard operating procedure one shrill answer to the murderous history of moderation.

ADVERBS

They are akin to the least important chess pieces but they lack, however, the workmanlike qualities and sense of self-sacrifice of the pawn, feeling that they have been unfairly treated in their attempts to become full-fledged verbs. Further, they resent their roles as backups for the muscular verbs—little more than scrubs or bench-warmers, those always chosen last in pick-up games. They also resent that they are often the first to go during revisions.

A KAFKA PROPHECY

Had he lived long enough some critics feel he would have been very attracted to the idea of writing a book about Bugsy Siegel.

SOME OF US

Remember how they made us sit with our hands folded, how whispering was a crime and passing notes so dangerous only the bravest or most foolhardy dared try it. They were testing us, we knew, hoping our spirits would break like the teacher's chalk. They said day-dreaming was against the law, but some of us escaped, slipping out windows and over cyclone fences, some of us flying away with heads like balloons. We taught our dogs to love the flavor of homework and became expert forgers of our parents' signatures. We knew they were teaching us how to die but some of us said no in our stealthy and stubborn ways.

ESTRANGEMENT

Have you noticed the way friends become strangers, receding along some long passage? First, growing distant, scarcely noticed, then their faces go vague, their features lost in a kind of haze, and soon enough they're far beyond earshot no matter how loud your shouts. They drew away? Were drawn away? No matter. It happens. And the next time you see them they have changed utterly and all night you implore the tip of your tongue to remember their names.

THE HOUSE OF NOT REMEMBERING

The streets that lead you there change their names without warning—Memory Lane suddenly become Amnesia Avenue which shifts quickly to Aphasia Boulevard. Persist though and when you arrive each room will allow you to forget whatever it is you came there to lose. First, there is a long hall with a minstrel gallery called The Dead. All memory of those you have lost rises and disappears on the dim strains of a lute and rustling leaves. Next are two rooms marked Stupidities and Embarrassments. A third, called Failure, is at the end of the hall and is the largest. There is a back bedroom where you may lose all recollection of insomnia, another erases passion or indifference, whichever has caused you the most trouble. Make good use of your visit because you will never be able to remember how you got there.

ADJECTIVES

Thought of as rather self-indulgent and even by some as decadent, they are in fact quite self-effacing creatures who are content to live in the reflected glory of nouns and are pleased to have some slight influence on them. In private they call themselves "excess baggage" and are grateful to still have jobs, subject as they are to the ruthless blue pencils of down-sizing editors.

HENRY AS IT WERE JAMES

The initial dilemma, and a lingering one to be sure, was to discover the exact amount that was required in a way more precise than is usual for one's epistolary missives in order to, as it were, divulge the information to foolscap, the, how shall one say, actual words rendered in serial form as the result of one's ratiocinative and mimetic faculties being employed to their, or very near, utmost—the design of which one has, in so many words, presented in some more or less fine detail in the proems, or should one say, the prolegomena or, not to put too fine a point on it, the prefaces to one's latter manifestations of narrative recreation of certain problems with the bipeds of the human persuasion may, with good or ill fortune, encounter along the thoroughfares of what some may nominate experience; therefore, having addressed the envelope, that action which is the very embodiment of the writer's esperance, one found among the accoutrements of one's writing surface—one's, as it were, desk—the proper number—to secure the delivery of one's not so much hallowed as periphrastic words to one's editor—of stamps.

THE LITTLE CIRCUS

It advertised the only trained hippopotamus in the world. We had to see that. It was Iowa and it was summer with all that oppressive heat. The tent was small and there was only one ring, the grass inside it scarcely trampled down—not a good sign. Early on we noticed there weren't many performers but they put on different costumes and took different names, too, for each of the acts. Part of the fun was to spot them in their new personas. The buxom bareback rider switched to tights and labored up the trapeze. We decided they were all one family. Finally, the hippo entered looking smaller than we expected—maybe it was one of those Iowa hogs in disguise. An older man, the catcher in the trapeze act, walked the hippo slowly around the one ring. It shuffled along looking none too happy and then disappeared through the tent flap. You asked, What's the act? What does it do? I said, I'm afraid we've just seen it.

NIGHT

Lately, night has shrouded the mornings with fog, some wispy version of itself, a lingering on as if it couldn't say goodbye to its dreams. Or is it only some lacy smoke from the dark's grim ovens?

I look out. The neighbor's porchlight is a tiny flower. Cobwebs hang from the leafless trees like worn-out negligees. But I feel something else—something lost, those dreams camped inside my pillow, all that's gone and can never be reclaimed. Even the sun loses today, too weak to elbow through the haze.

Gingerly, I enter the fraternity of traffic, headlights dim smudges in the fog, each of us steering away from thoughts of classic pileups—car after car dominoing into each other, flames finally burning off the fog and uncovering a scene from the war: Struggling refugees attacked by Stukas in '42.

POWER

Upstairs, asleep as another man, I sense myself
downstairs sitting late at the kitchen table muttering
and shuffling the drafts of this poem—the upstair's
doctor or lawyer's dim twin, the person he might have
been. Downstairs, then, I live the life he might have
lived while he sleeps his healthy eight hours and jogs
before breakfast. Of course he is who I might have
been as well but somehow I own him even though he
snorts that he could buy and sell the likes of me. But I
prove my case this way, quite deftly: It's time for
breakfast but he gets none—whose poem is this any-
way?—unless I write it in. Thus however rich and
powerful he may be he lives on my sufferance, eating
when I say so, sleeping when I write it down. But this
morning I relent and give him dry toast and tea while
I make myself a cheese omelet. Then I seat him across
from me in a faded sweat suit. He's haggard and in
despair (because I say so) and certain that his whole
life has been a mistake. I savor every bite of my omelet
before I write him off just as I did all those years ago.

BATTERS

I love the elaborate moves of batters in the on-deck circle. Those practice swings, the surgical application of pine tar, rubbing the handle with a bone, the swinging of the weighted bat. They also stretch and pull their muscles trying to make them into rubber. There is that way they take their stances—some digging a hole for their back foot, slowly and methodically fitting the shoe in the spot, some rubbing out the back line of the batter's box stealthily without looking at the umpire. They finally settle in and assume the masterpiece of a stance they've taken years to create—corkscrewed like Stan the Man, spread elegantly wide like the Yankee Clipper, with the bat label turned away —"I'm up here to hit not to read"—like Hammering Hank. All look like they've assumed an impossible pose and yet they do uncoil and sometimes even hit the ball.

BEACH

Somehow you're bound to come back as if to honor the salt dream of origin or some other crackpot idea. Whatever the reason, you return to the little beach town, the rocks, the abandoned lighthouse and that long stretch of sand where the dog sheds his leash and runs madly, where everyone, in fact, sheds his leash or just sits hearing summer changing in the surf. You love that roar, the drum slap as the waves come in, that muffled artillery, that swift retreat over and over. You come back for this: for theme and variation, for recurrence. You come back to check the first vision and find it still correct, your senses as wide open as ever and the sea's promise kept. And of course you bring the year's debris, the rubble of loss, twelve months of tired lumber. You also bring the broken hardware of failed mornings, the small change of winter light—whatever has happened and what has not. With all this comes the good and the bad and the mortar in between. You know your job is to lug all this to the sand where you bury the bits or scatter them or feed them to the sea in your ritual of forgetfulness. The aim is to forget yourself toward another year, forget yourself prepared with long walks and evenings, with days at windows looking for seals, watching kites and gulls fraternize. Strangely, you seem to dream it all—the year that spilled you slowly day by day until you came back to this sand and these rocks where you now refill everything that emptied with every bucket you can find.

THE OTHER

He lives on the other side of mirrors or continents
bearing some coded version of your name. He shame-
lessly steals your thunder but only in bits and pieces
so no one really notices. Then, however, he rises when
you fall, his summer becoming your winter and
because of him you live in a perpetual chill—icy in
July within those cold shadows he sends First Class
that shower you with the obscurity that keeps his lime-
light hot.

VOWELS

Feeling themselves to be the privileged offspring of nouns, they strut through our sentences, cocksure of their importance and certain that the language would collapse without them. (Decidedly xenophobic, they detest Slavic languages and Welsh, in particular, for obvious reasons.) They look down on one of their number and treat him with an aloofness nearly comparable to their attitude toward consonants which are, in their view, oafish peasants. The one they disdain? Why, Sometimes-Y, of course!

THE HOUSE OF THE PAST

> I wept over the smallness
> Of everything when I returned
> To my old village—
> —L. Reino Inala
> *After My Thirty-Year Exile*

The moment you get near your old hometown it inhales and grows smaller. There is, in fact, a real danger of permanent miniaturization—houses dwindling to the size of your old toys, say. The best advice is to stay away and let the old places work in reverse, burgeoning and ballooning, outgrowing your grandest memory. Its population will then explode from a thousand to millions and now, as long as you stay away, it will teem with life, people more numerous than the minnows you remember nibbling your ankles in the lake all those summers ago. By staying away your own piddling Main Street will become a vast boulevard with skyscrapers rising above the musty old movie house which will multiply to a thousand Odeons showing every movie ever made—even some of your favorites. The little town will bulge and your old four-room house will struggle up to mansion size, adding room after brilliant room, and you will even sense the few tattered dollars in your father's wallet transforming themselves into a great fortune.

REUNION: A SCENARIO

The scene: "Meeting a former friend." The two central characters wear uneasiness like a glove as their hands meet, shake, then fly away to the safety of pockets and secret fists. From a distance—across the room, say—an observer might think *Friends*, but nearer he would think *Shell* without quite knowing why. There should be the mustiness of empty houses in the talk— all furniture removed, bare floors echoing footsteps, corners heavy with memories of dead parties. The handshake as they part locks the door.

HANNELORE

All through your childhood she was like a rumor, a few hints caught in the aftermath of hushed talk, your mother suddenly busy at the sink, your father unduly interested in your school day. Remember how she turned up in only a couple of faded pictures in the album—a vague face in the background, sketchy features scarcely evident in the dim sepia. And though you have no direct memory of her presence your sense of her persists, a long skirt swirling out of the nineteenth century, a darkness, a sense of loss, a casualty.

Remember that car trip that went on longer than the usual outings? You knew it was serious because your father wore his suit—he kept tugging with his fingers inside the collar of his starched shirt. There was a hushed sadness inside the car, your mother speaking softly and your father driving without telling his usual jokes or commenting on the merits of the farmland you passed.

He stopped the car in a gravel parking lot in front of a large brick building. It looked cold and the windows seemed vacant as blind eyes. You knew she was there. Only your father went in. You and your mother walked around the small town and stopped for icecream in a little drug store. When you got back to the car your father wasn't there and then he showed up walking slowly and looking down, scuffing his good shoes through the gravel. After he got in the car it shocked you when he started crying. You had never seen him cry. "She's just not there," he said several times and drove off. All the way home the feeling in the car had the fuzzy sadness of Sunday nights when school loomed the next day and the frail freedom of the weekend was lost. Only it was worse than that.

Later, you learned that she had waited in Germany for seven years for her husband to make enough money so that she could join him in America. Working in copper mines and on roadgangs, he eventually felt able to take a homestead and sent her the passage money. You have thought of her days of waiting—the teasing from her brothers, the gossip in the town—and what her journey to this country must have been. We can't conceive such distances and hardships, complaining as we do when a plane is an hour late or the flight attendant runs out of those little packages of honey-almonds. A small woman in her twenties, she came by sea and overland without knowing the language, unsure of where she was going. She never deigned to learn proper English, in fact, which suggests the kind of half-world she lived in. The harsh winters, the childbirth, the fretting loneliness, watching her children become increasingly alien as they went to school and came back speaking words she couldn't understand, making fun of her old-fashioned ways.

Not long after you got married your mother told you about her wedding night. There was no money for anything like a honeymoon so the newlyweds stayed at the old farm and had gone to bed when Hannelore came struggling into their room with a folding cot and insisted on spending the night.

You remember dim bits of the farm—the house looming like a barn with cold-smelling rooms, rough floors, the attic where you found a broken castiron bank in the shape of a train. There was the thick light and the heavy odor of the real barn, too, and the threat of the irrigation ditch you had to drive over and the wide blond fields. You have glimpses of these but not of her. Something darker took her.

VIRGINIA'S LAMENT

All her life she sought a room of her own only to find at last that it belonged to Jacob.

HARDYESQUE

Visiting the Mayor's village in Wessex, a young woman attended a gathering at his house and in the course of the evening she was shown some pictures of the Mayor when he was a young man. She made much of them, saying how handsome he was, how much better-looking, in fact, he had been than her new husband. The Mayor had to admit that he had been a rather good-looking lad and his feelings unexpectedly quickened toward the young woman. The young couple soon returned to their home in London and while the Mayor thought of her occasionally he dismissed the flutter of warmth he had felt in her presence. My goodness, she was married and besides that she was far too young for him.

Then the day came when he heard in the village that the young couple were due to return on a visit. He arranged for a gathering to which they would be invited and then pored over old pictures of himself, finding several that he was sure she had not seen. During the party at his house the Mayor found it hard to show the pictures to the young woman because of the largeness of the gathering and his duties as both Mayor and host. Suddenly, however, he saw that she and her husband were about to leave and he grabbed the stack of pictures and stumbling toward her said, too loudly he realized, that he was sure she would be interested in seeing these. She gave them a cursory and rather bored glance and then handed them back to him, giving him a puzzled look as if to say, Why on earth do you want me to look at these tired old pictures?

CARPE DIEM

This morning he knows exactly what he has to do—it is all very clear and so simple it surprises him—and he packs his gear with great care. He wears his freshly washed and starched fatigues and feels as sharp as he had in the army, boots spit-shined, belt buckle glistening. Moving briskly as he works he likes the ozone flavor of the autumn air and the pure blue sky which seems as clear as his plan. He thinks again of leaving a note on the fridge but knows his plan is far too complex to spell out in words however clear it seems to him. Later, his wife and kids will understand. The plan simmers just above his heart and he is dead certain that it is right. Today will be a great day.

In spite of having drunk malt liquor all night he feels sober, reflexes in perfect order, eyes and fingers in ideal harmony. He drives along his usual route, not speeding, enjoying the light traffic and the purring gurgle of his pickup at stop lights. He thinks of his job, remembering those abstract motions, that lifting, bending and rising, the dance that danced its mania into him is gone now, invisible. He feels no anger about it. *They'll understand*. He takes it as a good omen when he finds a parking slot easily and at the time clock he loads a clip and slips the safety off and decides to hell with the foreman and just opens fire.

GOING BACK TO WORK

The furnace goes on again, a low music that starts and stops like its opponent, the refrigerator. How they both sing with the washing machine! And on the radio the singer's voice breaks so extravagantly so many times it makes no sense and no clear word cuts through the cracks.

Among these sounds we have our love and we talk late of promise but remember the confetti of malevolence the fools scatter on our path. All those cop souls out there who seem to wish nothing but illness and disgrace on us. In fact, tonight it appears such wishes are our country's favorite crop—or at least the most loved hobby.

We know our love grows weeds beside the railroad tracks or dimly between the pavement cracks. But this is our crop and we nurse it along tonight and every night hoping it will persist however doomed it seems. This is why we encourage every weed we see, coaxing each one up through the cracks our sidewalk offers like a great river's million tributaries.

THE END OF A YEAR

This one ends in summer. It began in June. When August fails it disappears, lost in albums of evanescence, the wispy message of some long dead fire.

But now we rate it, weigh its micrograms of meaning, those swerves made toward love, those accidents of anger. But was it good, you ask?

Some days it welled high, other days it swam dregs without oxygen. It was a year.

But such disclaimers aside, honoring our god of irony, we assert the year was good and name it so but without trumpets, quietly, yet with whispered hosannas in the dark and sweet curses for our enemies whose wild envy was honed just right this year.

Envy with a razor edge is dangerous but this is, we're sure, a good thing, too. They must be careful how they handle it.

PERFECT ATTENDANCE

This morning's paper seems like an exact copy of yesterday's—yes, even the crossword puzzle is the same which is a real disappointment. In spite of that I find the puzzle impossible to do, my memory not being what it used to be. The politicians on page one are spouting the same old guff—surrender and we'll kiss you full on the lips. Or is it kill you? They never make it clear, deliberately, but it's a safe bet to expect the worst will win—you know the ones filled with all that passionate intensity—their ballot boxes stuffed like Thanksgiving turkeys.

I think this is even the same cup of tea I had yesterday. Certainly it's very cold. I don't know why I bother. Plainly the radio is singing the same songs and the calendar is a joke—all those numbers adding up to nothing new. Even the weather is a Xerox of what happened yesterday. Rain was promised. It isn't raining again today. So much for promises.

So much for news and songs and tea. So much for you, so much for me. You see how carefully I divide the boredom equally in my sing-song way but still there are no takers. All the others think this is a brand new day—"New thresholds! New anatomies!"—full of possibility and rain and spring flowers even though it's October. I know those flowers very well: They were here last year. They never die. They just go on blooming in an ecstasy of ennui. Actually, I'm sure it's just some trick, some *trompe l'oeil* trumped up by the politicians.

And this egg in the egg cup seems very familiar as well. I think I even know its name. I think I went to high school with this egg. Her name was Dolores. She

74

sat next to me in Algebra I. (Or was it Civics II? My memory goes on acting up.) All I know is that neither of us learned our lesson though she did get a certificate for perfect attendance. She was never late or absent in four years! Quite amazing. I should get a certificate, too. I've been here every day. I've even done my homework, rereading the same newspaper rather too thoroughly every morning and learning everything by heart except the crossword puzzle. (What the hell is a Celebes ox? A mine entrance? A Polynesian goose?)

But why do I sit here remembering my classmate, an egg named Dolores? She had very pale skin and never missed a single day. In spite of that everyone said she was a good egg. I have my doubts, though. I wonder if she still has that certificate. Did she frame it? Did it get her a job as a time clock? Or an egg timer at least?

Cold tea, stale news, stale tea, cold news. And, hell, this is exactly the same morning when everyone thought Dolores would finally be absent. We knew she had broken both legs and an arm doing homework the night before. We were sure there would never be enough king's horses and men to get her to school that day. But just before the final bell they wheeled her in, complete with IV and respirator. "Here! Here!" old Dolores wheezed and Miss Jones yelled, "Atta Girl!" waving the attendance book like a checkered flag at Indy. The boredom of it all was nearly more than we could bear.

O Miss Jones! Where are you? I'm here, too. Wave your book for me, just once, as I chart my voyage through the overly familiar furred hours. Hello, Dolores! I'm taking another crack at the crossword and even trying to read between the lines of this damned paper. I'm doing my best but it isn't easy. Rain is almost falling, Dolores, and flowers are straining hard to be individual as fingerprints. Got your homework done, Dolores? How has your attendance been lately? Mine has been perfect but I'm still waiting for my certificate. I promise I'll frame it.

THE HOUSE OF LOST THINGS

When we think of a place for lost things we usually imagine some catchall drawer of string and dull scissors or old love letters and warranties for long dead appliances. We all have one like that though we rarely find the mundane thing we need in it—the AA battery, a bolt for a nut. No, the place I mean is far beyond single socks and gloves, lost buttons and ancient greeting cards. It is in fact a house like a vast drawer which holds all our unspoken words, things we didn't do as well as the things we did, all the lies we ever told along with those times we bit our tongues when speaking out was dangerous. Here if you look hard enough you'll find the crumpled map leading back to innocence, another leading straight to guilt, laid out step by step, and the forgotten route to remorse. All the documents are gathering dust—moldering blueprints, dead agendas, even the certificates that prove us human. But this house is very hard to find, its address unknown, the place where dead letters thrive. It holds the shopping list of everything we never got. But it's all there if you can find your way—forgotten dreams like mildewed valentines, what we once knew so well but lost, those logarithms of the spirit, the apocrypha of redemption. Somewhere in this huge space is the answer to the story problem of our lives and why things worked out so easily once and why we wound up like this, always looking in a quiet frenzy for this lost house.

BEING INVISIBLE

The first thing is that it's not at all as you thought it might be at twelve or thirteen—all those chances to see naked girls. As time goes by it's finally just a bore. You see everyone but no matter how fast you dance, no matter how gracefully you spin, no matter, in fact, how sweetly you sing, no one ever notices you. As for nakedness—most people look better with clothes on.

THE HOUSE OF FEAR

Here every floorboard creaks in an ominous foreign language and the windows shudder in your spine. The very walls sketch out the plans of assassins with their zigzag cracks. And within the labyrinths of those walls diseases hatch, misfortunes too harsh to think of hover near the ceiling among the cobwebs. After midnight there is a roll call of every childhood ogre and they crawl from under beds and out of closets, their claws scraping the pillow beside your ear, their hot breath fogging your windows.

APPROACHING 1934

This time you have to travel in reverse—remember
the way people had to back up muddy hills in their
Model-Ts when they drove home from April dances?
Reverse was the only gear strong enough to make it
over those hills. Or maybe something is just rewind-
ing your story that's been going on fast forward lately.
There are those clicking sounds but they may be the
crank of the old car. Yes, they are. And then you adjust
the magneto though you can't quite remember what
it's supposed to do. Could this be a dream—a new one
unlike that one about having to go back in the army?
But you're spitting blood and your nose feels numb.
Yes, the fight. But it was nothing. Some insult winding
up behind the dance hall. You do hate those red flecks
on your white shirt though. The motor grabs hold and
the car shivers and coughs with impatience. Strangely,
you know every twist and turn of the gravel road, the
moon riding high and bright as chrome. But then you
get lost—that rewinding whirr off to one side, or is it
grasshoppers? A curve jumps at you like a deer. And
where are your pals? They've melted away or fallen
out. But they left the jug and you take a pull, nearly
gagging at the razor blade taste. In the army dream
you're thirty-five or forty-four, hopelessly protesting
that you've already done this but no one listens. You
wind up wearing baggy fatigues in a dismal barracks.
But this time it's different and you find yourself at the
last hill just before home. You straighten your tie, try
to flick the spots off your shirt and choke down the
last swallow from the jug. You have no idea of who
will be waiting for you at home but feel you must look
half-way presentable. You turn the car around so you

can use reverse up the gumbo of the hill. And this is the way you enter your old life—backwards, wheels spinning and fishtailing toward the crest where your whole past stretches out before you in a steely dawn light. Or is it your future?

THE PROBLEM OF THE SKY

Unless it does something special—lightning, thunder, snow—we don't give it much attention. It's just there like a ceiling or a hat that fits so well you never think about it. Looking up now I see the clouds but never remember their right names so I call one Roger, another Spot. I also see them as George Washington or sheep or ships which is an exercise that's becoming as boring as the ritual of sunsets—which are fakes these days anyway, sunlight mixed as it is with toxins and sentimentality. There is of course the night sky with its stars but mainly we save them for vacations at the beach where motel owners have cornered the market. Dawn? It looks best when you've been up all night.

ON THE TRAIN

The nearly featureless landscape had the austerity of a Mondrian along with the tough emptiness of a Hopper. But the key thing you learned from such a scene, so seemingly bereft of interest, was that any detail is important: an abandoned tire, a piece of paper, a fallen branch...

THE ASTROLOGER

How can you tell if the astrologer is mad or not?
What he says makes sense, sort of, or we dearly want
it to—futures he gives sound so much better than the
ones we feel we are destined to have. We also feel we
deserve the ones he gives us. So we listen to what he
says, trying to look skeptical but mainly looking goofy.
What are we doing here anyway? But if he's wrong, so
what? It kills the time and we feel flattered by his
attention.

THE HOUSE YOU LOST

You ran an errand so long and intricate that you lost your way home. No one noticed your absence and you kept forgetting your way through the world. It was the kind of adventure you expected—diners and a lot of yawning. But it went on such a long time—trees turning anorexic, your summer shirt too flimsy in the cold. You stole a blanket from a clothesline. You slept under bridges. You drank sweet wine with your new-found buddies until your teeth loosened. Then one frosty morning you found the list of things to do in your pocket and completed your round of errands. When you got home no one noticed.

From PARAGRAPHS

Are you genuine? Or merely an actor?
A representative? Or that which is
represented? In the end, perhaps you
are merely a copy of an actor...
                                    —Nietzsche

Urgent action is not in graciousness
it is not in clocks it is not in water
wheels. It is the same so essentially,
it is a worry a real worry.
                                    —Gertrude Stein

Experience is one of the forms of paralysis.
                                    —Erik Satie

LUNCHROOM

The knives on the table are there for a purpose, but their true function has been forgotten over the years. Actually, the lunchroom which now appears so calm and civilized is an arena, the trays and tables converted shields, and we who sit so quietly are gladiators. The man who cleans up, the one who looks so dull, grew tired of the mess and cleverly diverted us by serving food to slice and eat, thereby satisfying our need to use weapons, which he stealthily reduced in size until they now seem innocuous, just as he had assuaged our desire to kill by teaching us the rudiments of gossip.

LATE AT NIGHT

Not willing to exert the mind enough even to sense the quality of the lives nearest us, we will, however, late at night, create from scratch around a few random sounds in the cellar—pipes knocking, the furnace working—a whole human being, the prowler come to punish us for lack of love.

MY DANCER

My dancer stands still most of the time—like an anchor. In fact, his feet leave the ground only when he hoists himself into bed. Your dancer may spin and jump. My dancer sneers and says, "I hate sweat!" His background? Close-order drill at Fort Benning, trick knees, poor wind. Here are a few of his dances: The Dance of Spilled Milk and Burned Food; The Morris Chair Polka; The Tango of the Coffee Urn; The Linen Closet Schottische; and, his masterpiece, The Coma Mazurka.

SIRENS

Just now they moaned as they always do. They are in pain when someone presses the button which is for them like an exposed nerve in a bad tooth. So they scream until the pressure stops and allows them to sink back to what they like best: silence, moisture beading on their lips, darkness.

THE EMBARRASSED

You see a woman you know, and unaccountably, you become embarrassed. You stammer and can't wait to get away. It is only later that you remember: yes, last night you were together—in your dream. The next time you see her you look closely, eagerly seeking some hint of embarrassment in her actions.

INFANTS

Many speak of the looks of wisdom infants have but there is another quality rarely mentioned: the melancholy amusement in their eyes. This look arises from resignation, which, in turn, results from the infant's uncanny politeness, a politeness profound as sacrifice. Faced with an existence of possibilities without limits, the chance to be a lamp post or an ode or an inland sea, the infant, with infinite compassion for its parents and a deep understanding of compromise, more or less agrees to become a child.

GUILT

We sense a criticism, possibly overhearing it as we walk, and immediately we begin rearranging our past to fit the crime we suspect we are suspected of. By the time we reach home we have altered our history, discredited all alibis, documented and labeled evidence, and, opening the door, we begin to serve our sentence.

GOLF

Though they seem carefree and childlike, golfers are, in fact, very sinister. Their ease and playfulness is merely a cover-up, a very clever one, for their darker aims. You may have noticed that newspapers occasionally print articles telling of people who have been injured or even killed by golf balls. Following such reports you will notice golfers grow restive and self-conscious. They are afraid they will be found out because the whole vast apparatus of golf has been developed to accomplish a single purpose: assassination.

HOUSES & SHIPS

The houses are ships—run aground so long ago no one remembers—continually assailed by pirates. Because the times seem to have changed, the pirates now use disguises—their hooks and peglegs and big gold earrings are concealed by nondescript uniforms. But the boarding parties go on, made up of what appear to be paperboys, milkmen, and that ominous figure in gray who brings the mail.

BODIES

Given their natural inclinations toward betrayal, they cannot be trusted. They introduce foreign elements into our lives; they encourage appetites we exhaust ourselves resisting or satisfying; or they develop their own vices of the cells which we call disease. And since we have only their little hands to work with, we are helpless against them.

PROFESSORS

Many talk of dedication, service to youth and knowledge, scholarship and independent inquiry. This sort of talk is quite simply a ruse. Professors are voluptuaries of the dull and the real masters are those who conduct themselves so cleverly that no one ever discovers that their dullness is, in fact, a brilliantly feigned act.

WE

We travel a great deal but are never welcome. Our bags disappear, conductors shunt us away from reserved seats, waiters and other officials look at our money as if it were stolen and at our faces as if they were those of terribly defeated candidates. Lateness becomes our way of life, but we are not hated, only distrusted the way men are who request small loans in order to gamble or buy cheap wine.

THE ORTHODOXY OF ROUTINE

We are told the age lacks faith, that no permanent values exist, that the world is unstable, but many, let us call them the heroes of punctuality, who would follow a dogma if it existed, have circumvented the problem by making of their routines, protocols, schedules, and agendas a watertight doctrine which they always adhere to, as they say, religiously.

FRIDAY AT 4:30

Moons and pies sit around a table talking about their ingredients and chuckling over moon-jokes and pie-jokes. "Gooseberry" gets a big laugh. So many things happen! Adding machine unrolls a list of funny numbers while the sticky tongues of manila envelopes wag with pleasure. Test tube talks about urine samples and nudges syntax in the definition. They all chant, "Gracious! Oh gracious! Such fun!"

THE ART OF THE WOODCUT

There is a great deal to be learned about conduct from this art. First, a decisive thing is done to an unblemished surface, the tool makes a clear deep line, and because of its general similarity to a pencil line the amateur often thinks of the work as drawing until the print is made. Then he learns that the whole untouched surface is what is really like a pencil, strange and blunt to be sure, and that, further, everything has come out backwards.

THINGS

There is in things a silent insistence we usually manage to ignore. There are, for example, those long rails carrying trains or lying still during the coldest nights of the longest winters.

THE TALENT HUNT

Stooges wait everywhere on high stools like tennis judges. They stake out spots in all the drugstores looking for blondes or hang around schoolyards and bus stations. They listen a lot and nourish themselves with mint-flavored toothpicks. At the same time the talent waits in lobbies smoking three packs a day, tans fading, skills going stale—pawned, withering in guitar cases. Busboys and carhops, the talent bends whichever way it's asked, giving it away, looking for *the big break.*

THE HARMFUL STATE

Nearly everything you see inspires suspicion. Little signals speak of the ominous future the world has in store for you. But this is only the condition of optimum health, indicating that, like a cat, you are wary. Such a state cannot harm you. The harmful thing is not to suspect but to know.

From LITTLE-KNOWN SPORTS

In La Mancha province I possess seven and a half acres of quicksand on which I organize sinking contests...The rules are simple...the last to disappear wins.

—Pierre Bettencourt

I'm no stranger to the temptation of the flesh...I confess that I give in almost daily (except Fridays when we have fish)...

—Gunter Eich

For what do we live, but to make sport for our neighbors, and laugh at them in turn?

—Jane Austen

IN SHADOW

Off to one side, under the leaf shade, I spot myself staring toward the snapshot's deckled edge, curious apparently about something going on there, some marginal event, perhaps even a stranger passing by or a dog on a dog's serious round. I've forgotten the lens and closed my ears to the photographer's directions and stepped back into the shade while the others, all strangers now, practice their various poses, each trying to win whatever prize it is that photographers seem to offer. The strangers work hard at it, showing their teeth of different sizes and conditions, squinting quizzically, or raising their eyebrows with all the supercilious aplomb of eight-year-olds. So eager, so sure to win while I have done everything possible to take myself out of the picture without actually walking away. I still wonder what moves beyond the stiff margin, lying low behind the thick leaves that shade the house, watching.

THE PHOTOGRAPHER

You see him at every party, outfitted like a soldier with cases and tripods and those subtle lenses he likes to fuss over like a nanny. The shutter opens and closes so many times it seems to breathe and everyone readily falls into a pose when he nods. He likes this. He likes to nod and watch people vainly try to reveal their good sides, just as he likes to escape early with the evidence, the event rolled tight and secret in the camera's dry interior.

With the evidence in hand he loves the alchemy of darkrooms—the liquids, the close darkness everyone must honor on pain of exposure. And he loves the mystery as pictures reveal themselves—fools' faces suspended in foolishness forever. And the marvelous thing: He is guiltless! He was no fool among fools. The others asked for this, they posed! They loved the music of the shutter and their own faces betrayed them into these grotesque images, their very skin his accomplice. He loves these moments and generously sends as many prints as you want.

MADAME AUPICK

This is her only known photograph. She is seated on the porch of the "Maison Joujou" at Honfleur. She wears black and seems to bar entrance to the house which rises around her with nearly perfect symmetry, a house like a well-structured book. Rising from what appears to be gravel or crushed seashells are seven steps, one for each sin, leading to the place where she sits. To enter the house you will have to ask her to rise and it has been too long—she will never rise. She will bar your entry forever, tiny as she is, dwarfed as she is by the "Maison Joujou"—which one suspects is merely a façade or, at best, one large cold room containing a single candle and a crucifix. Even through a magnifying glass Madame Aupick's face, in her only known photograph, has no features at all.

OROFINO

Orofino was the unspoken rumor, the waiting for letters, the bad news ready to happen. It was the place my father's stolen childhood lived, where denial waited to deny a final time. Everything not given would not be given once more. A whisper, a foggy postmark, a smuggled name faint as the circles of late night coffee cups as I ate my cereal. It was sachet and camphor, the feel of something hidden, something made of lace soaked in cologne. It was the dark bedroom beyond memory, the name Orofino. A meaning on a shelf just beyond my reach. An object the opposite of the hidden gift, some present that crumpled inward like a toadstool, ever inward and deeper into wells deeper than our lake. The gift that was the absence of gift, the gift that took away, that ate, that demanded and denied. The gift that spent itself, that hollowed out, that drained light from the day. Orofino.

MONSTERS

We are surrounded by monsters each day, but we
have taught ourselves to move among them graciously,
almost as if drugged, and never take note of their fea-
tures. They do the same for us.

HIS SABBATICAL

Routine has won and he wakes every day at the same time, then enters the dim brotherhood of drivers—each mounted behind glass. Still, he dreams between classes, writhing in the office where the radiator sweats and plots behind his back. He travels far, every inch of red tape snapped by his sprinter's chest. He strolls a ship's deck, talks of horseflesh with retired colonels in the bar. Ashore, he climbs mountains and follows unknown rivers to their source as easily as you move your finger in the phone book. He looks at sights and forgets them immediately and takes pictures with the lens cap on or throws the film away. He needs no record—this is life, he is there! Sometimes he finds a village where the Americano is loved by everyone and he writes a novel quickly, making no typographical errors. He hobnobs, his passport and his body stamped with royal seals, and goes from monastery to orgy freely as a milkman in the steaming tropics of that radiator.

SALT AND PEPPER

Monogamous as wolves they move through their lives together, rarely separated. To honor their feeling for fidelity we have developed the habit of asking for them together, knowing that they keenly feel any separation, however brief. Though salt is our favorite, a relative really, we never indicate this in order to spare pepper's volatile but delicate feelings.

DUST MOP

This creature is some curious by-product in the evo-
lution of the unicorn.

TABLES

They are faithful as dogs and, like dogs, consider themselves central to the household. "Fundamental"is the word they use. Their hierarchy is intricate with, surprisingly, the dining room and kitchen tables looked upon as rather stolid beasts of burden—good fellows but rather stupid oxen finally. Coffee table has some status, comparable to that of lap dogs, though end tables rank rather higher, having as they do only one task— holding a lamp or ashtray in place, for example—while the occasional table by virtue of its very name has dreams of possibility and is thus respected as a near member of the leisure class, but for utility and absence of labor coupled with an unending supply of gossip, the bedside table remains at the top of the list and nearly all the others aspire to his role.

FLOWERS

They are birds which spend their whole brief lives yearning for the sky, but they have planned their careers badly, going for bright plumage but no wings. A few do make it miraculously to the wallpaper where they become fossils, but most, finally recognizing their true condition, pluck out their feathers as quickly as they decently can, knowing the last one will say "loves me not."

BROOM

Like the feather duster it feels incomplete, a creature only half-evolved, and anxiously scurries everywhere trying to find the rest of itself.

COBWEBS

Over and over they try to spin the single thread that will lead us safely past the minotaur and finally free of this labyrinth. But they suffer from nerves—they drop a stitch, they panic, and in desperation refer it all to a committee, which produces this result.

IN THE NATURAL HISTORY MUSEUM

Whole armies of birds sit tensely on lacquered branches ready to fly south at any moment, but winter never comes. In another area tooled leather alligators sun themselves and try to digest dinners of kapok. Near them the pottery relic of a giant turtle's back exhibits the tracings of a stylus which outline the basic tenets of vague and pagan religions. (His jaw is set firmly as a prime minister's in time of war.) And the whale, whose true skin is reputed to be no thicker than the film on boiled chocolate, lies on a painted wave, his great flukes silent as the rusted cannon in the park.

SLEEPING

Though winners are rarely declared this is an arduous contest similar, some feel, to boxing. This fact can be readily corroborated by simply looking at people who have just awakened. Look at their red and puffy eyes, the disheveled hair, the slow sore movements, and their generally dazed appearance. Occasionally, as well, there are those deep scars running across their cheeks. Clearly, if appearances don't lie, they have been engaged in some damaging and dangerous activity and furthermore have come out the losers. If it's not dangerous—and you still have doubts—why do we hear so often the phrase, *He died in his sleep?*

CRUDITY

Oddly enough timing is crucial to this activity in that a particularly crude or boorish act must, to be successful, be observed. In isolation it scores no points at all or, at best, may be interpreted as an act of vandalism. Further, the appropriate audience is necessary and such audiences are not gathered easily. Thus a whole congress of qualities is required if one's effort is to prove effective and receive a decent score, the most essential of which is, inevitably and obviously, finesse.

TEDIUM

This clever invention of the playwright Anton Chekhov has burgeoned over the years until it is now, among amateurs, one of the major activities of the middle classes of the Western world. The more experienced dress in black and tell people at random that they are in mourning for their lives over and over, in order it seems to induce tedium in their listeners. The more earnest participants, however, twiddle their thumbs a great deal and sigh deeply as afternoon descends into evening. Dinner for them is always boring and entertainment an absolute affliction. When someone is told he has won the contest for the day, he yawns.

GETTING LOST

This is an activity that has about it the subtlety of Zen and can only be managed by thoroughly experienced travelers or, at the very least, long-time residents of a particular neighborhood. The simple aim is to get lost and in doing so feel those emotions of doubt and strangeness, alienation, and, yes, even panic which, for the experienced player, is especially exhilarating. The trick then is to accomplish this deftly within familiar surroundings, areas that are literally known like the back of your hand. The venerated masters are those who are capable of getting lost a few doors from their houses. All aspire, however, to achieve the truly legendary feats of the revered grand master who is reputed to have gotten lost every day for a year though he never left his easy chair. Such genuine mastery is humbling indeed, but needless to say it is also inspiring.

HANGOVER

The competition here is fierce and long, but few records have been kept just as few competitors ever truly witness another's score. This remains secret—a ballot no one marks—though there is a good deal of talk about it, like fishermen describing the one that got away. The true player simply endures whatever the previous night has given him. Cheaters, who are frowned on if the true player is capable of a frown, resort to a hair of the dog. True players hold such actions in contempt while they stare into the metaphysical distance and move with great care through the morning hours.

SMOKING

Like cock fighting or pit bull contests this is rapidly becoming an outlaw sport though many still engage in it rather openly and with a certain nervous bravado. There are some as well who practice it surreptitiously in forbidden rooms and elevators. Others practice it in private as single consenting adults.

STUPIDITY

The competition here is enormous—a daily Olympics in fact—though certain guidelines have been ineptly drawn up over the years. Still, the burgeoning numbers of contestants remain a genuine problem, but the guidelines which prevail, scrawled ungrammatically and illegibly, seem to indicate a means of classification which helps to limit the number of contestants. The main groups are, first, politicians, then administrators of all types, followed by generals and editors.

GETTING INTO BED

Some approach this with indifference, misunderstanding it as so many misunderstand the daily. Others, however, approach it with the care and attention to detail of mountain climbers. There is about their actions an air of ritual as they give this nightly activity its proper respect. Once they have prepared themselves physically and outfitted themselves with the proper equipment—bed, mattress, sheets, blankets, pillow and case, alarm clock, etc.—they approach the bed matter-of-factly.

For the act itself several techniques are available. There is, for instance, the Fosbury Flop whereby the participant sits on the edge of the bed and rolls backward and to his right, aiming the back of his head at the pillow. Another method is the Western Roll—a swift knife-like leap under the covers. Some practice variations of the scissors stride, and there are also rather baroque freestylers who try to ring changes on the established methods. All approaches have their dangers and if not conducted properly the participant may spend a sleepless night, or, worse, may miss the bed entirely and suffer a painful injury. Though it is a less demanding game many prefer to play doubles which has its virtues.

LYING

In that you can have any number of opponents this can be a very difficult endeavor, requiring as it does an intricate, double-entry method of keeping score. The truly excellent, of course, juggle their score cards with ease, knowing as they do so that the real problem lies elsewhere: In order to lie successfully you quite simply must know what the truth is. As philosophers have persistently told us this is no easy task, and, because of this, there is some reason to believe that the truly outstanding liar lies out of a strong sense of modesty.

BEING WITH IT

Sunshine is a good example. Having come of age in 1968 as Betty Lou Balloon of Odessa, Texas, she immediately changed her name to Sunshine. Lately she has achieved one of her primary goals, allowing her as she says, to actualize her potential. She is the proud possessor of a loom and a word processor. She now works fairly steadily on the former and needs the latter so that she may like share her health food recipes with her sisters. Thus far her only original recipe is one for macramé and cheese.

DELIBERATE MISUNDERSTANDING

Obtuseness is often confused with its counterpart, deliberate misunderstanding. It is an unfortunate confusion, mixing up as it does the clear definition between the professional and the amateur, artist and hack. The obtuse performer, for whatever reason, simply does not comprehend, whereas the performer who deliberately misunderstands *knows* but pretends not to. The tragedy, of course, is that if the latter is found out he loses his professional standing, but if he is not found out he is simply branded obtuse.

VERN RUTSALA

A Handbook for Writers, Vern Rutsala's tenth collection, contains new work and selections from *Paragaphs* and *Little-Known Sports.* His other books include *The Window, Laments, The Journey Begins, Walking Home from the Icehouse, Backtracking, Ruined Cities,* and *Selected Poems.* Among awards for his work are a Guggenheim Fellowship, two NEA Grants, the Juniper Prize, an Oregon Book Award, two Carolyn Kizer Poetry Prizes, the Duncan Lawrie Prize, a Pushcart Prize, the Northwest Poets Prize, the Richard Snyder Prize, and a Masters Fellowship from the Oregon Arts Commission.

The Marie Alexander Poetry Series

꠸

Series Editor: Robert Alexander